A LITTLE GUT MAGIC

Matthew Lippman

NINE MILE BOOKS

Publisher: Nine Mile Art Corp.
Editors: Bob Herz, Stephen Kuusisto, Andrea Scarpino
Art Editor Emeritus: Whitney Daniels
Cover Art: Devin Martin, "Plenty of Fish In The Sea," 3x4 feet, oil on canvas.

The publishers gratefully acknowledge support of the New York State Council on the Arts with the support of Governor Andrew M. Cuomo and the New York State Legislature. We also acknowledge support of the County of Onondaga and CNY Arts through the Tier Three Project Support Grant Program. We have also received significant support from the Central New York Community Foundation. This publication would not have been possible without the generous support of these groups. We are very grateful to them all.

ISBN-10: 1-7326600-0-X
ISBN-13: 978-1-7326600-0-7

ACKNOWLEDGEMENTS

Some of these poems have previously been published in the following places:

Ploughshares: Watergate

The New England Review: King Stuff

American Poetry Review: The Happiness Pain, Fuckin' Shit Up, How We Become Our Fathers, The Ignorance Of The Rain That Is Its Delight

The Academy of American Poets, Poem A Day: Slowly In Prayer

Green Mountains Review: Speak American

Subtropics: Disappear Like An Owl

Seneca Review: Perfect Time, Fishing At Wegmans

The Literary Review: The Light

Redivider: The Pretender

Barrelhouse: When The Cicadas Were Out Of Their Fucking Minds

The Chattahoochee Review: Annual Physical

The Georgetown Review: Savagery (winner of The Georgetown Review Prize)

Horsethief: Tip Tap, Wastebaskets Of Pink

Bateau: Ants and Birds, Citrus Bombs Of Love

deComp magazine: Live Things In The Road

Souvenir Lit: That Nutjob Word, One Big Immigrant One Big Immigration

I would like to thank: Michael Morse, Rebecca Lippman, Naomi Laguana, Sharky Laguana, Eliana, Natalie, Alex Gould, Daniel DeLeon, Tina Cane, Dore Kiesselbach, Juan Felipe Herrera, Matthew Dickman, Aaron Tillman, and Jessica Levine. A special thanks to Josh Rilla for his keen eye and attention to detail. A huge thank you to David Weiss, for being there at the beginning, and giving this manuscript a sweet embrace.

And, of course, to Rachel, for all the big love and support, always.

TABLE OF CONTENTS

For Naomi, Sharky, Billy, and Tommy

PART 1

A HUMMINGBIRD OF YELLOW SEX

My wife sends me links to family photographers and musicians.
She sends me blogs of elephant caregivers and painters who believe
    in metal.
There are 400 texts about the color red
and a sizable file on the way Israelis chop garlic and Palestinians
    peel potatoes.
The last voicemail I received from her was 15 minutes long.
She started telling me what a dipshit I was,
and then she started telling me that Donald Trump's facial hair
smells like overcooked eggs,
and then she told me we need a new fax machine
just in case the internet burns down.

Right now I look out the window and there are 2 cop cars cleaning
    up a car crash.
The trees have no leaves on them,
and I can see a banana floating between one building and the next.
It just hovers there.
It's a banana hummingbird,
but there are no flowers for it to suck,
no nectar to devour.
It is what sex looks like.
I stare at it.
I stare at sex,
at the banana that is sex that looks like a penis
and then opens up and looks like a vagina.
It's right there between the buildings,
a hummingbird of yellow sex.
I want to throw away the phone, burn it down,
all the texts and the voice messages, burn them
down.
I want to go home to my wife
and start a fire.

THE HAPPINESS PAIN

What am I supposed to do when the wife is at Target and Trump is
    in office?
I hang blinds.
I buy bullets. I don't really buy bullets.
I think about buying bullets to stave off the unhappiness pain.
My daughter is upstairs singing *Don Giovanni.*
She doesn't even know it's *Don Giovanni.*
The problem with *Don Giovanni*
is that it is opera.
If it were a pop song that Stevie Nicks wrote,
Trump wouldn't be in office. That's probably a lie.
What's not a lie is that my wife would still be at Target
with the big red shopping cart
racing around the aisles
trying to beat back her mother's imminent death,
trying to beat back the sadness in her heart
so she might fall into it,
right there in the toothpaste section.
I hang the blinds to keep the light in.
To keep the wolves out.
They come to my neighborhood every Sunday
in the form of Russian Orthodox parishioners
who pray at the church across our street.
I love them when they are across the street.
When they are on my side of the street,
their fangs drip with blood and wolf spit.
I hang the blinds to keep them out,
and the president out,
and all the president's men, very much,
out.
When my daughter sings *Don Giovanni,*
my face hurts from happiness.

When I put the screw in the wood
I try and stay with that pain,
the happiness pain,
where it does not matter
that the color of your shopping cart
is the same color
as the liquid that drips off your teeth
and stains the carpet.

LIVE THINGS IN THE ROAD

There was a carnation in the road.
I ran over it.
Like the way my friend Jackson ran over the squirrel.
It was in the road.
He swerved left and smashed the thing.
Neither of us said a word.
The sky just kept on being the sky.
When I ran over the carnation,
I wished I lived in New York.
I could get on the 2 Train,
take it from 96th Street to Borough Hall.
No more driving. No more
rolling over live things in the road.
It makes no sense to me,
the desire to run over things.
My whole life I've thought I was a nice guy.
A guy with radiators for lungs.
A guy with soft hands.
But there I was doing 30 on route 9
and the flower just showed up.
Gotcha, I said,
looking in my rearview mirror
to see it flattened.
The way the squirrel was flattened,
everything red
and red
and even more red than red could imagine red being.
It's a thing we all are at some point—
crushed on the roadway, crushed in silence,
crushed red in love.
This is the problem
or not the problem.

It's the thing.
The thing in the roadway smashed
that has to be held.
You have to go to it,
stop the car, get out,
get down on your knees with it
hoping the oncoming traffic won't get you in the process,
knowing damn well
it will every time.

WATERGATE

It's 11:02.
I was supposed to take the kids outside at 10:13.
My underwear is over my head.
I'm trying to sniff out the boy I once was,
my private parts tiny and nutmeg.
I didn't give a shit about Superman.
I was in love with Watergate.
Watergate was my super hero.
All that corruption. That darkness.
Those men in black suits, greasy hair, on television,
who lied and lied and lied.
I'm trying to sniff back into my best form—
the 8-year-old who loved the end of Nixon
instead of taking the kids to
ride bikes that they don't want to ride,
eat melon off the rind like spider monkeys in heat.
I inhale, exhale,
and it's there, that sweet smell of *young boy,*
of Downy, of New York City 1973.
All that dirt and sweat.
It's there. I can smell it.
I take lion breaths. I take hippo breaths.
When I was 8, no one took me outside.
I tossed a rope from the 3rd floor window,
repelled down in my Nixon mask,
met the boys at the corner and blew up Manhattan
with wheelbarrows of Spanish, English, and Chinese firecrackers.
Eric had the Haldeman mask; Karl, Agnew's grill,
and the best one of them all, the John Dean visage—
that mixture of mayhem and music,
of innocence and regret. I inhale. I exhale.
I can't get my kids out of the house.
Get out of the house, I scream at them, my purple boxers draped over
    my face.

Find some trouble at the corner store then get out of it.
Make some mischief then be contrite.
Get lost on the bus and find your way home.
You can do it. I promise, I say,
without anyone getting hurt,
without anyone's feelings getting hurt. It's 11:18.
I was supposed to get the kids outside. But I'm breathing.
I'm sitting here in the kitchen with my drawers draped over my
    face,
and I'm still breathing.

SPENDING MORE TIME NAKED

The world says,
Get naked,
so I do.
I go up to the attic, lay on the rug with my arms and legs stretched
    long
into the long hours of the night.
It's a long stretch, like the stretch of Miley Cyrus
when she sings Melanie.
It's the run and roll of Ariana Grande
when she belts out Crowded House.
I am that naked.
It's the naked of cohabitation and fuck the poets.
Fuck the wind farms and the gypsy moths.
They are here again, and I'm taking off my clothes.
You can hear them crunch under the sole of your boot.
I get naked to hear them squish under the heel of my flesh.
That's not what Noel Gallagher taught me
or God
or the 1 year old down the street, Emmett.
He's naked all the time—in the ocean,
on his father,
between the scooter and the dream of the scooter.
For me, it's the world rubbing up against my ribs
saying *take it off take it off*.
I listen and say *okay okay*.
Talk to it, the world says.
So, I rip off my shirt and socks, my shorts and drawers.
What's up? I say.
Naked says, *How do you like me now?*
Truth be told, naked never sounded so good.
The body is the best thing no matter how many grapefruits you
    squeeze,
no matter the size of the television with all of its crazy color.

Tonight I am up here in the attic with my ass against the carpet,
my thighs rubbed up against the wall.
I've got my feet up and my armpits soft.
It's a long night into a long stretch of naked.
A perfect pop song of naked.
A three part harmony of skin on skin on skin.

WHEN THE CICADAS WERE OUT
OF THEIR FUCKING MINDS

I tried to imagine myself on the other side of Prince but couldn't do
   it.
That's the truth
because Mark Heyert took me to the little record shop
next to the Smith Opera House and bought me *Sign 'O The Times*
like it was the last thing anyone could ever do.
Oh, you can't even talk about that record, not even now.
You can't talk about the way Mallorie Evans kissed me
outside of Miller Hall
when the cicadas were out of their fucking minds
trying not to die.
It was September and who knew there'd be that much grief in the
   world.

Tonight, maybe there's that much grief in a guitar
quiet in its case against the heat.
I slung one across my shoulder once
to see how it felt
in the crook of my back
before I threw it off the porch
to see
if I could get it to vibrate into the ether,
so the hair on my neck would convulse in 4/4 time
or in the off-time of the off-beat
the way it did when I heard *Housequake*
for the first time.

I'm quaking now with the rest of us.
I don't care who you are
or where you hide your drugs,
pray to your God,
lift your child before the sea—
this is worse than we could have ever imagined.

I tried to imagine myself on the other side of Prince
after he left this earth today
but can't quite seem to do it right
except when I hold Heyert's hand
on the banks of Croton
looking west across the Hudson
to a dream that still lives out there, somewhere,
of all things good and beautiful—
wet pink petunias,
a woman and a man between a mountain,
and a woman and a man between a mountain.

There is only this
and the memory of Mallorie's lips
sliding across the night
to stave off the death march of those unruly insects.
I wish she were here with me now, Heyert too,
in his big white caddy screaming,
Not your momma,
not your momma,
not your motherfucking momma,
to push the death back
so Prince could have one more day
to pick up his purple guitar,
to let us imagine
what we have always imagined—
that a man and woman and a mountain
on this side of Prince
is the better side to be on,
the 17 year old cicadas--
billions of them about to burst forth from the earth,
and rise from dead.

TO GET OUR DISASTERS OUT

I don't want to talk about how black people and white people eat
    spaghetti together.
I don't want to talk about how Kim Jun--whatever the hell his last
    name--
is so not like Tracy Morgan it gives me a headache.
I don't want to talk about the power of headscarves
and how all the Jews can't figure out how to live peacefully with all
    the other Jews and then all the other people on The West Bank.
Talking about poverty in Soweto and Harvey Weinstein's penis
gets me down
even though I'm writing it down.
What I want to talk about is
Joan Armatrading's voice on *Come On Home.*
I don't even want to talk about it.
I just want to listen
to her.
Or, Joni Mitchell's dulcimer between the leaf piles,
the ones I raked with my kids.
We messed them up to get our disasters out
but no one got hurt.
Not even the leaves.
They just went up in the air and got caught in their hair
and came down.
I want to talk about the way they got caught
and that they left them there all day.
It was tree day in the house
and they were trees.
They picked apples from one another.
They got forest happy. They got shade insane.
They got that sound trees make
at the top,
the canopy,
when the wind blows and you know the silence is magical,

that it lives inside of you,
and it makes you want to say something beautiful
but you know better
and don't.

THE LIFE OF THE MIND KICKED OUT

The mind walks into a bar, sits down, orders a scotch,
a single malt,
pretends it wants to be sophisticated,
looking for something outside
that used to make the inside
feel smart.
But there is no more scotch.
There is no more single malt.
The mind looks around for someone to talk with.
Everyone is either too drunk or too drunk.
The mind is not sure what has these people drunk.
The mind wants to talk Rilke.
Wants to talk Lester Bangs on *Astral Weeks*,
then spend an hour listening to The Lion's Share show in August
    of 71,
how it was playful in an e minor chord harmonic groove
that was both an angioplasty hubbub that tried, ever so sweetly,
to quell the domestic turbulence that was outside,
raging on the streets,
between the cops, the politicians,
and those radicalized hippies who, years later,
made fortunes off their facelifts.
For the mind, it's all gone.
The life of the mind kicked out of the brain
into a swellstorm of nonsense,
a shitstorm of howdy doodie dum-dums
pulling levers on Pennsylvania Avenue
that open trap doors.
There go the poor people.
There go the blacks and Jews.
The Mexicans and fags.
The gays and queers,
the transgenders and the transmissions of tenderness

that used to move the mind into bedrooms before sex.
The mind sits down at the bar and orders a street choir
or a bandstand
only to be met with a drum machine and an auto-tune tambourine.
Remember when we sat up till midnight talking bicycles and Beethoven,
how the roving madness of Foucault caught our eye before we knew what to see
and the lilacs made us swoon?
And when they made us swoon, it was then, and only then,
that you took off your clothes and I took off mine.
The mind is talking to itself again
and the bartender offers a Labatt's.
It's all that's left.
Cheap beer and no one to lend an ear,
engage in an ensemble of back and forth.
The mind has had enough and does all that it can to get drunk
then gets drunk,
passes out with its mindfulness on the bar until closing
and then it's closed,
the bar, the barstool, the bartender.
In the morning, curled up against the curb, it thinks:
We used to talk before we made love.
We used to talk for hours
and then we made love
for hours
and then we slept.
It was a good sleep,
a restful slumber,
you and me and the whole country
like anything was possible,
like possibility was your mind and my mind
that made a whole new mind between us
which was a body
that we could reach out, and, if lucky enough,
we could touch.

ANNUAL PHSYCIAL

I swear, I sat in the MD's office with the 80's Pandora station
pumping out hits by A-HA and Bryan Adams,
Cyndi and the Tom Tom Club.
I said, Doc, I refuse to let you
stick your thumb up my ass
to check for monsters.
Thing is she was psyched.
Like some great weight had been lifted from her chest.
So, we went out to Lab Tech room
and took my blood,
pints and pints of my blood,
Madonna piping in over the speakers,
a little Lionel Richie for good measure.
It was the best medicine.
Your BP is good, she said.
I said, Your BP is better,
and we spilled my blood across the floor
to paint pictures of bison and aliens on the wall
as if they were the same thing.
Take mine, she said,
and I stuck the needle into her vein, softly,
and the health of the planet was never better
even though we both knew that in 100 years
there'd be no penicillin to speak of.
There'd be no ADHD or Xanax or even cancer
so we cranked up *1999*
into Howard Jones
into Grace Jones
and our lab coats were Technicolor
and she was Joseph
and I was Joseph
and our eyes were ablaze with possibility, with hope,
because the bison had leaped from the walls

and the aliens had landed their spaceships
on the table with all the gauze and empty test tubes.
You could see the joy in their faces
for smashing it all to pieces,
and it brought joy to us.
You see, she said,
you don't need me, medicine, or diagnostics
when we have this,
and she was right,
and I was so glad I had said no
to her latex covered thumb
while *Eye of the Tiger* morphed into *Bette Davis Eyes*
and the dance kept on getting better and better
with each discarded syringe,
each rainbow colored mask
littered with germs.

THE PRETENDER

I used to try and play this old piano.
It stood upright in a corner by the back door under a skylight.
The keys were not finely tuned and sometimes the pedals did not
    work,
but I pushed anyway.
I sat for hours and knew the chords with my right hand
but couldn't do shit with my left.
I pretended.
For hours I played one song pretending
I would perform it in front of 100,000 people
in an open meadow in Glasgow or a field
just outside of New Paltz.
I have been pretending ever since.
That I know how to fix a carburetor,
kill large numbers of ants when they run rough shod through the
    kitchen,
kiss my daughters before leaving for work.
I pretend that I know how to make money and spend it on organic
    broccoli
and inexpensive sneakers with the blue stripes.
And love; forget about love.
It's a masquerade, a con job, and most days I don't even know how
    to say hello
without someone else's face covering my face.
Yesterday it was the face of Brunel, from Roslindale,
and the day before that, Steve Jobs, although he is dead,
and I hate technology.
This morning, it's Elton John.
I tap these keys like it's a piano and think that this poem is
    "Levon."
It's that old song from the 70s,
the one I spent hours trying to play on that old upright
shoved in the corner where all the sunlight came.

It ripped through a skylight and illuminated my body when I was
    naked,
when I was dressed in feathers and sequins,
when the crowd went wild
even though I had no idea what my right hand was saying to my
    left
running up the keyboard trying, like broken birds,
to fly.

A UNITED STATES OF AMERICA POEM

The United States is still here.
That's why you have to go kiss your kids before they head out to
    the school bus.
That is why you have to go out to the dead tree,
cut it down,
rip up the stump,
plant a new tree,
maybe a Japanese Maple
because the Japanese Maple is red
and America is still here.
It's in the bedroom, under the bed,
next to the plastic bin with all the summer tee shirts,
the blue one with ponies on it,
the same ponies that run and up down hills in West Virginia and
    Cold Spring, NY,
the ones you rode as a kid
when the air smelled of sweet lilac and burgundy autumn.
You fell off of one once,
landed on America, and America picked you up
like a grandfather who still had his strength,
put you on his knee,
and rubbed your cheeks to make you feel new again.
That America.
It's still here in the ignition of the car,
you've just got to go find the keys and fire her up,
4 cylinders or 6, it does not matter.
It doesn't matter that the mudslide in Big Sur
which crushed Highway One
crushed Highway One,
you can still get America going again,
drive over the stones and smashed trees to the other side
where the ocean goes on forever,
where America says hello in waves and sea glass

and hints at revolution.
You know that revolution,
the one that means well for the guy at the farm-stand
and the gal in the office with the big windows,
the revolution of a man with no home
and the woman with no food
that still believes in the belly of the day,
that there is a word called *yes* that will lead her to a door
and that she can,
with her last ounce of strength,
turn the knob and walk through.
It's that America that is still here and it lives in your heart.
The one that beats so strong you have to kiss your kids
before they head out for school with the lunchboxes and lunch
    money
and provided lunch service—the apples, the apple juice,
the turkey sandwiches on wheat bread
with the crust cut off.
It's an America for today, the most necessary today,
where Georgia and New York, Vermont and California and Idaho
    and Paris, Texas
have all gotten together like old friends reunited,
sitting at the river on cotton blankets
not talking.
Not even listening.
Just being united states under one sky.
It's blue. It's not red or white.
It's a blue sky
and it's here where it has always been.
You have to believe this.
You have to go outside right now and find it.
It's easy.
Just look up.

PART 2

ROLLING DOWN THAT WINDOW IN ROBERTA FLACK

Everybody's got something to say about something I say.
I am not saying I have anything to say
but it feels like every time I open my mouth
there is another mouth
trying to get into my mouth
to mess it up.
Switchblade the teeth.
Tourniquet the tongue.
Hey, wait a minute, I try to say, it's just words.
It's me just making words--a blacksmith of words
making horseshoes of sentences.
Makes me think I should just shut up.
Let Roberta Flack do the talking
except she ain't talking--
she's whistling, moaning,
singing as slow as a blade of water
rolling down a rain soaked window.
It's love. It's the kind of love
I wish I knew in my life
even though I have it in my heart.
Everyone's got something to say about that, too,
but they don't know what to say. It's just there,
that blade of water rolling down the window in Roberta Flack.
She's the only one who knows anything now.
She's the only one who knows how to talk with her dashiki and her
    piano.
But, I am far away from that.
We are all far away from that.
That's why there are hurricanes.
That's why the water on the window
smashes us to bits.

ANTS AND BIRDS

Coupla ants show up.
Coupla dead birds.
The kids bring them in.
The cats.
There's nothing I can do about any of it.
My heart breaks all over again
when we kill the ants.
When the cat plays basketball with the birds.
I hug my kids. I yell at them
while the rug is disinfecting itself.
You think it's funny?
It's the worst thing ever.
Across the street
the churchgoers pray for their silent death.
They pray for their silent life.
I want to walk over to them with my shoebox filled with the ants
    and the birds.
Instead, I stay quiet
and gather the kids.
Let's scream, I say,
and we do.
At the top of our lungs.
We bring down the light fixtures and the ceilings.
We bring down the sky.
The cat is so freaked out
he runs to the basement
where his stash of mice and flying things linger in corners.
We are so loud the fire trucks come,
but when they come we are quiet.
We no longer sound like sirens and are silent for all the dead things
    in silence
and for all the live things in life.
This is family life for us.

The ants are dead and the birds are dead.
They have no tribe, no pack, no litter,
no landscape in which to scamper.
We should be sad. We should be happy.
That's not what happens, though.
What happens is we lose our minds to combat the breaking of our
    hearts
and then it gets too much
and we just let our hearts break.

SAVAGERY

There are all these people with so much going on.
The fat lady coming out of the gas station in her Ford Explorer
with three kids in the back,
smoking a Pall Mall and I'm like, *Lady,*
slow down
but maybe she is slowed down and what the hell do I know?
There's the guy mowing his lawn across the street
who I had no idea, until the other day,
was a cop
and busted gang leaders in Brighton
for selling hookers and crack
to Saudis across the sea.
For all this time I thought he was just a guy
with an Asian wife
who loved his rhododendrons
and had no kids.
All these people and I should watch my mind
the way you should watch your mind
when you see me pick up my kid around the belly
and drag her upstairs
because she lied about the cookies and the tomatoes on the wall
and the sadness in my heart.
What do you know?
Do you know the sadness in my heart?
What do I know?
Do I know the sadness in your heart?
And that is why I have to be careful
when the mailman tosses my mail across the front steps
because earlier his big brother was diagnosed
with a rare form of cancer.
It's a special place this planet
with all of its high power lines and cell towers.
It's a godly visitation of blueness

that we might have turned rust color.
On my way to the Roche Brothers for some kosher beef salami
I see:
two kids on skateboards,
a bi-racial gay couple,
the haircutter from Iran,
the Italian cook and his sweaty bride.
We don't know till we know
and even then we don't know.
So, what *do* we know?
The only thing I know is that there are all these people
and so many more people
and people at the beach,
thousands of them in their beach chairs,
inside their sun screen and buckets of watermelon
and beer
and it boggles my mind
that we are all here, together,
with the lions and cheetahs and bears,
all bloody and spitty and, for the moment,
perfectly at peace.

YOU COULD PLAY IN TRAFFIC AND NOT EVEN WORRY

We saw an orange and black bird
then my nephew almost got hit by a car
riding his skateboard down a hill
into traffic
his brother yelled Billy
at least they both wore helmets
my daughter screamed Billy
she just had her head on
then the bird screamed Billy
and the cars in traffic slammed to a stop
the bird flew into a window
but was alright
everyone was alright
I keep imagining a whole world
where everyone is good and fine
in orange and black
we'd all have these wings and skateboards,
helmets even,
but they'd be just for show
because our hearts would be that good too
and even when we flew into windows
and cars almost hit us
we'd be good
there'd be a goodness so big
you could play in traffic and not even worry
the cars would be that soft
and so would the tree trunks and the neighbors next door
even people on bicycles
who you think don't like you
they might not like you

but they tolerate you
softly
the way the anxiety
about getting a new job college heartbreak
is softly
as soft as the orange and black winged blackbird
that flew past Billy and Tommy and Natalie and Eliana
standing in the street
stopping traffic
they were traffic cops
soft traffic cops
kid traffic cops
cousin traffic cops
their wings so big we need more of them all day long.

HOW WE BECOME OUR FATHERS

My father did this thing once--
we were walking the walking mall in Iowa City,
between Washington and Johnson, maybe,
who can remember,
it was so long ago it has no name.
He did this thing
where he tried to leap frog a small light pole in the middle of the
    mall.
It was Thursday or Saturday
and there was a herd of people shopping for pants.
It was September and wanting to be June.
He's a short man, Mel,
and when he put his hands out, propelled himself up,
his body did not cooperate and
he did not clear the black steel rod,
fell right on his face and, I swear, you could hear something inside
    of him die.
He must have been 50, 51,
and I was trying to write poems and my folks were divorced;

there was my father
splayed out under the Iowa sun like a frog pinned in Biology lab
and I wanted to run so far away from him
into the brick wall behind me--
disappear into it--screaming
I do not know this man I do not know this man,
but didn't and could only offer him my hand.

Later, I could not remember what freaked me out more—
watching him fall or my reaction to watching him fall.

Today, on my walk into school,
I tried to flip a glass iced tea bottle from one hand to the other

and the cap flew off
and the tea showered itself all over my blue shirt
and the bags I was carrying unloaded on the earth
and there I was
a hot mess of my father,
myself, 50, 52,
I can't remember.
It was Thursday wanting to be June,
and I wanted to run so far away from myself,

and scream *I do not know this man, I do not know this man,*
hoping that I might meet my father in there
with some shard of love
inside the red rock
and that maybe, for once,
on a hot July day wanting to be August,
we might actually get the chance
to be more alive than we've ever been and
break each other's fall
before we actually hit the dirt.

FISHING AT WEGMANS

I went fishing at Wegmans.
Threw my line in.
Came out with two guppies and an Alaskan roll.
Purple Rain piped in through the store speakers.
I thought of my friend Matthew.
He's got a baby on the way.
Reading books called *The Elevated Child*.
Books called *To Find A Thumb*.
My tackle box was filled with lures,
with night crawlers from last year.
In the pineapple aisle
I was all wet.
What were the dinner options?
At Wegmans you can buy a beef tenderloin for 50 dollars,
stick it in the oven,
feed a family of 6 for 3 days.
They pipe *Purple Rain* through the speakers to elevate the child.
On his way to a new life
I will send Matthew a Cornish hen.
My heart is so lonely I put waders on,
wade further into the refrigerated store.
Prince's guitar breaks me in half.
When I think of Matthew
I can't help but to think about myself.
This is my problem.
If I had a baby on the way
I would devolve into a bear.
An elevated bear.
Wade into the fish aisle with my black fur and white fangs,
stick my face into the freezing Alaskan waters and get me some
    salmon,
real live Sockeye, swimming into their death.
Fuck it, I think, and do it anyway,

Purple Rain purpling up the white waters, the pink flesh,
my children 7 and 12. They don't care.
The thing about kids is that they don't care where you fish.
I don't have a baby on the way
but the rest of the world does.
They're crying from hunger and it's our job.

PERFECT TIME

Miles Davis says that Prince has perfect time.
He said, *I have perfect time.*
Then I saw the movie *Arrival*
about those aliens who write sentences
that are three dimensional or six dimensional,
rich with nuanced antediluvian lovesongs
of geothermal proportions.
I still can't figure it out.
Something about time as a non-linear spider-web,
bent,
forward and backward,
an inside and outside layered happening.
If we lived in that kind of world,
on that slippery sphere
what might Miles have said about Prince and time?
What would perfect time look like?
A guitar solo that sung outside the beat
wrapped inside a tree
that he sat under as a child
in burnt out Detroit?
Would there even be a beat?
A place between the beat?
I'm just wondering because I have to pick up my kids at 4,
go to the dentist at 5
then be home by 6:30 so my wife can make her 7:15
with the chiropractor
and my pants feel really loose in the waist.
They feel like they are going to fall off
and I'm going to drop down in the mud
in the barnyard with all the cows watching.
It doesn't scare me.
Secretly, I want the mud all over me—
my face and ass,

even inside me,
my mouth and nose, my eyes and ears—
like a primordial alien creature,
half of this world, half of some other world
where time's perfection
is stupid-sloppy-messy
and will always be Prince's left hand
slapping Miles' right.

SHAME

There was this girl, K.
When she was fifteen I said, K.,
Your nose is a ski slope.
She liked me.
She wanted to kiss me and hold hands to the bodega,
buy a Malta, sit on a stoop at midnight,
whisper against the burn of taxi cabs.
It was fun to be loved or wanted
but I did not want to love or want back.
She lived on the 15th floor in a building in the 20s
and we smoked pot.
She wore long wispy paisley dresses.
It could have been 1972 but it was 1981.
We smoked pot and could see The Twin Towers from her window.
Let's jump out of your window, I said,
and fly to the East River.
I might have been high or pretending to be high.
Then I said, *Your nose is a ski slope,*
and when I saw her 20 years later
at a café on 8th street between 1st and 2nd
I said, Hi K.,
and she looked at me with a knife and blowtorch.
New York was a different city then.
There were more drunk people with a lot of money.
The planes had flown into the towers.
The horror was stapled to lampposts in photographs of the missing.
Each one was a Tower of Babel.
Each one was a teardrop filled with marigolds and acid.
You wanted to stay away but you couldn't.
K. worked in a café.
It was messy and busy and I wanted to say I was sorry.
Say, *Sorry,*
but it seemed so stupid.

All you had to do was go outside and listen to the bits of paper
fly across the river into Brooklyn and then back.
I wanted to say,
Can we please go back to your apartment?
You can put on your dress.
I will take off my shirt and we can kiss.
We can kiss and kiss and kiss.
Or, I can just shut up and go back to the way it was before.

THE PRESIDENTIAL TOWERS

Dear 70th Street off of West End,
there was a day when you could see Jersey from the corner.
There was a balcony on the north side of the street
with a view to Iowa.
A corner apartment with windows that went on forever.

Dear West 70th Street,
I used to park my red Honda between your shoulder blades.
I used to kiss Bonnie beneath the streetlamps.
She told me Cicely Tyson lived on the 10th floor.
Do you remember when Miles held the keys to her front door?
I rode the elevator with him once,
or is that just a story I tell at dinner parties
when I am lonely?

West 70th, when I was boy there was a girl.
When I was a young man there was a young woman.
We kissed beneath the street lamp that lit up 1983 like Jupiter.
She lived in The Presidential Towers.
It is 2016 and Cicely Tyson is 91.
Miles Davis is nowhere to be found,
though I find him still
in every elevator that wants to go up.

Bonnie, when the bulldozers came to move the dirt down the
    block,
you had gone to the back part of your mind
where endless boats bobbed
on the currents of the Hudson
and you wept.

70th, did you weep when they went up, down the street,
those new buildings with all that glass?
When there was no more river to watch?

Did you stand under your streetlights and hail a cab, a cop, a
    construction worker
who knew all the best cat-calls?

It's late now with nowhere to go
and I am on your corner
in the corner of my mind
where there is only that balcony.
We stand on it in the dark New York night,
naked, after lovemaking,
and the river is still very much ours.
It stretches out to Jersey and Iowa and way beyond the city limits.
It makes us feel that we are presidents of our sex,
our hearts,
and the dreams that young people have
who are very much a part of something beyond the balcony.

Tonight, we are a country together
on West 70th in an apartment
in The Presidential Towers
and the street light of your street
floats above our heads like we are angels--
and we are--
and we turn to return to the bedroom,
to sit down in the secret world of your rug
and make laws that will change this land forever.

PART 3

SPEAK AMERICAN

I've tried to speak American.
All my students are from America.
One is from San Paolo. One is from Oslo.
They speak beautifully American to one another in Swiss and
    Portuguese.
I tried to talk to the Dominican in Spanish but quickly realized
the only words I knew were curse words.

The most American thing I have ever said is *I love you*
but that's more international, even in space.
I slept in a sleeping bag with my 10-year-old crush
under the stars in upstate NY
and when she touched my neck I said, *Mi amore.*
I had seen Sophie Loren in *Marriage Italian Style*
and under that canopy of flickering light
believed I was a Sicilian love queen movie star.
My crush crushed my heart two weeks later in her American accent.
She said, *I don't love you. I love John Henry.*

These days I wonder if being an immigrant is the most American
    thing you can be. Saying *the immigrant* is not politically correct.
Saying the *non-dominant tribe* is always the tribe you don't belong to.
I want to belong to the *I Love You Tribe*
so I can kick all the poets in the ass and say, your next book will be
    called
The Book of Be Nice. Who wants to be nice anymore?
The lawyers don't,
and the drug store owners who used to own local drug stores
but got crushed by Walgreens. That's talking in American. Being
    crushed.
Not saying a single word.

ONE BIG IMMIGRANT ONE BIG IMMIGRATION

The ferry from Battery Park to Ellis Island did not make me cry.
Then I put my face into The Registry Room tile
and remembered the crocheted print of my grandmother at The
    Wall.
My wife asked if she'd ever been.
I could not say no or yes.
I had a Brian Blade ballad in my head.
But I was still on the ferry
and Natalie wanted to watch the waves.
Where are the dolphins?
Was the sea of New York Harbor
as dirty today
as it was when my wife's grandfather looked over the rail?
He was 4 from Poland and had the rickets.
History is always a myth
even though it is the truth.
You have to remember your name is Dolphin, I say to Natalie,
even though it is Natalie.
You are always that smart and can swim thousands of miles
on your own
to get exactly where you need to be.
She looks at me like I am a madman from another world.
I put my face in the tile
to conjure the smell.
All that human stink.
All that 15-day steerage up in the funk.
No matter how bad it was,
I can hear Brian Blade's *Bluebird*
falling out of my whole body onto the floor.
We are all boats.
We are all the inside of boats--
one big immigrant,
one big immigration

on *The Lady Liberty,*
The Gateway,
*The Ms. I Am Going To Get Some Action In This Damn Town If It Kills
Me.*
And there it is, New York,
that big sweatshop of cash and corruption,
across the harbor
waiting for me and my family to return
with the rest of the Asians and Germans,
the white ladies from Missouri,
the Muslims speaking French.
Everyone with a camera. Everyone with a charm bracelet.
I want to shout. We were here first!
But, that's just because I am sad.
I have my face in the tile and it is weeping.
My wife's grandfather is in there with me.
My grandmother. All of Poland—
the stink of poverty and piss.
Truth is, I am glad my kid gets to ride on this boat
and not the other boat.
I am glad I can play her Brian Blade
when we get home.
It's right across the water
no matter how many steam ships I take
up The Henry Hudson Parkway
onto I-95
deep into the hills of New England
across the Atlantic
and into the shetls of Transylvania.
My face is in the tile,
and no matter how bad it smells,
it is the stink of nowhere
and it is very far away.

KING STUFF

When I turn 49 I will turn 50.
I will have a decade plus one year
to make a million dollars.
I am not joking about this.
I want to go to Barcelona with my children
and dance Flamenco on the Spanish Steps
then come home and have three plumbers
fix up the upstairs bathroom with butterflies and nightingales.
I want to introduce myself to a side of myself that I have never met.
The millionaire.
If you visualize something does that make it come true?
It's so beautifully, what,
Buddhist? New Age?
I hear people say it all time—*visualize it
and it will happen.* I tried.
I saw myself as an ogre under a bridge in Manhattan
and I was that ogre,
but only kinda.
I was more kinda too kind
at the end of the day and the ogre project failed.
Once, I visualized myself as Willie Mays,
but I could never get black enough
or enough from Westfield, Alabama
with a mitt on my right hand
for any of it to, you know,
feel correct.
Every night I go to sleep and see stacks of money that smell exactly
   like money
in my living room.
I see a chair from Crate and Barrel on top of those stacks
and there I am with a crown, and a white robe with the fur collar,
the king of my millions. King Stuff.
I look at me and I look gross.

It's so much easier to see myself as gross and be gross
than to be a king on a stack of money in the living room
while the kids play with matches and light the whole thing on fire.
Most days I open up my eyes and start to sing.
My daughters taught me that.
My wife too.
Most days we get out of bed and croon about
the millions of bottles of dollars on the wall,
while we hold hands and fall over the furniture
laughing our asses off.

THAT NUTJOB WORD

At the meeting I said, *We need to talk more about solitude.*
Everyone looked at me like I was crazy.
I said, *I am fucking crazy, yep, that's right.*
Then I remembered this dude who is actually crazy, Ned.
We were in a seminar together.
I said, *Blake was a mortal nutjob*
trying to piece together the tapestry of his mind
as the visions got better and better.
Afterwards, Ned said,
You can't say that word.
I said, *What word?*
He said, *That nutjob word.*
Then he went into the bathroom
and looked into the mirror. There were dragons coming out of his
    eyes
that he tried to stuff back in
with toilet paper
but nothing worked
so he disappeared into the back of his own swallow
and drowned.
Solitude can kill you sometimes.
Sometimes, when you are all alone in the stillness of the evening,
sitting in your rocking chair after midnight,
the thing will come up behind you
with a leather belt
and choke the shit out of you.
Most times, it'll just hold your hand
and you'll hold its hand back.
You'll be an active participant in your solitude.
That's what I said at the meeting--
We need to be active participants in our solitude.
When I shut up
the trees from outside slid through the windows

like the dragons that slid out of Ned's eyes.
But I was no nutjob
and did not need any tissues to fend them off.
They just came in quietly and sat beside me
listening with their tree ears
and their tree hearts
like we had done this a thousand times before.

THE IGNORANCE OF THE RAIN
THAT IS ITS DELIGHT

All I want is the rain,
the Bill Evans and Joe Pass rain.
The rain that soaks through my car windshield in minor 5ths
and walking crescendos.
The rain that rips my face off in missed notes,
bleeds its wet into my neck and laughs
when I am down on my knees.
It's raining in Antarctica and we are doomed.
It's raining in my daughter's belly and there are more children.
There is nothing to stop the deluge of Louis Armstrong 16th notes
and the birds that want to die in my cat's mouth.
They don't know that they want to die,
but it's raining in their death.
Bill Frissell knows this in his upright bass
and Jackie McLean under the covers
with the little devils of horror
nipping at his toes.
We've all got those little numbskulls running through the night
straight for our face
to remind us that whatever good we do
there is more good we can do.
The rain recognizes that it is rain.
It rolls over itself.
It is raining in Antarctica
and we should be scared.
My daughter is scared when the windows are open
and the thunderstorms come and won't fall asleep.
I say it's Anat Cohen's clarinet rain.
I say it's Art Blakey.
The whole thing--from grey cloud to lightning bolt--
it's Blakey rain.
She looks at me with her crazy rain eyes and finally falls asleep.

I have done my job.
It's the job of the rain--
that it makes sure that we do our job.
That is why you have to get up out of bed every day,
walk out into the sun and muggy day
and do your rain dance.
With all your flowers and your feathers.
With all of your spices and fertilizer.
Get outside and boogie woogie to make it rain.
Dance till your face comes off,
till the rain comes and gives you a new face,
a snake face, a Thelonius Monk face,
filled with deep rivers
and waterfalls that won't shut up.

FUCKIN' SHIT UP

They're fuckin' shit up again.
The guys in yellow hard hats.
Right next door. They have their dinosaur teeth clacking.
Their pink overalls juicing. They're juicing up
the walls with jackhammers,
jamming their knuckles through tile.
I want to join them
but left my nail clippers back at the house.
Lemme give it a go, I say to the foreman.
But he's a forewoman and tells me
I don't got what it takes.
What does it take? I ask.
An absence of self, she says.
But I'm already gone, I say.
The walls come down, the splinters of stone fly.
You come out of your momma knowing how to bust your ass
or you come out of your momma in the fetal position, she says.
I can't figure out what is a who anymore,
where is a when.
I've fathered girls, I say.
She says, The sun mothers the moment.
I want to fuck some shit up, so badly.
The roof tumbles. The shingles shatter.
Please, I say,
let me break something to build something.
For whom? She says.
And I don't have an answer.
Or, the answer, like on most days, is for nothing.
But why can't it be bigger than that?
Nothing squared times infinity squared again.
So I bum rush the job site and wield my blowtorch,
heat up the joints, the bolts, the steel.
It's some shit getting fucked up.

Like a factory whistle blown, cutting the still air,
or the Big Bang, cutting infinity to pieces.
I mean wasn't that the biggest meanest fuckin' shit up there ever
    was
and we're still trying to wrap our heads around that one?
It won't work, I say, and figure on it.
That's why I want to be part of the littlest smallest fuckin' shit up
    there can be.
That's what I tell her, the forewoman in her yellow hardhat,
raging hammers against the stone,
needle nose pliers into the belly of stars.

SLOWLY IN PRAYER

To be thankful for the Starbucks lady, Lucy,
who is pissed at me for asking too many questions
about my damn phone app
is one thing.
To be thankful for my wife plastering my face to the bathroom
    floor
with pancake batter
for missing the bus
is another thing.
I tried to be thankful for my eyes this morning
even though one of them is filled with pus
and the other with marigold juice.
Marigold juice is the stuff that comes from the flower
when you put it between your palms and rub, slowly in prayer,
even though nothing comes out.
It's the imagined juice of God,
the thing you can't see when you are not being thankful.
I try to be thankful for the lack of energy that is my laziness
and my lonely best friend with no wife and children
knowing I am as lonely as he
with one wife and two daughters.
Sometimes we travel five minutes to the pier in Red Hook
and it takes hours in our loneliness to know, in our thankfulness,
that if we held hands it'd be a quiet romance for the ages.
I'll admit, I'm thankful for Justin Timberlake
because he's better than Beethoven
and my friend Aaron
who lived in the woods with an axe and never used it once.
I try hard to forget love,
to abandon love,
so that one day I will actually be able to love.
Until then, I am thankful that Lucy wanted to spit in my coffee,
or imagined that she did,

and thanked her profusely
for showing me which buttons to push
and how to do it, with just the right amount of pressure,
the whole tips of all my fingers dancing like stars
through the blackness
of a mocha latte, black, no sugar.

PAPAL DREAMS

Can I be The Pope for a day?
I want to dress in white robes and be Papal.
I want to walk through the projects of Detroit
and the poverty fields of Darfur
with no selfishness.
I want to ask for forgiveness of the little kids with cancer
and the mules who have been beaten up the trail.
Is there a way I can get me some of that Vatican vibrancy?
I'm so tired of dialing up the ego doctor
for my prescription of *love me* pills,
exhausted by the need to be recognized by the newsman
and the publishing house
and the woman down the street who runs the bakery of spelt bread.
In the morning I walk to the snow-fields and undress myself.
The cold dances on my nipples and makes them hard.
Even here I think about my body too much,
that this will be a good story,
that someone will listen when I tell them
I stayed too long and frostbite set in
and gangrene
and then my vital organs ceased,
but I lived.
Glory me.
Most days all I think about are my kids, my wife, my book, my
    award, my next circus
in which I will be my ultimate ring master.
All I think about is *my my.*
Does the Pope believe he is master of the universe or just God's
    voice?
In doing good deeds is there a way to remove oneself from the
    goodness?
I would ask him this if we were in a pool hall playing nine ball and
    drinking Schnapps.

My intentions are excellent, I would say, I just have this need to be
   noticed.
I am tired of this need
but I love getting it met.
Perhaps I will fast, I think.
Perhaps I will genuflect.
Perhaps I will walk the Himalayas
with a sack of water and three moccasins.
But, this is a different life I was born into
and I am not that strong.
Even for one day.
For one day I will call myself Pope, even still, but only to myself,
and then I will go bathe the world's soot
from the backs of my children's necks.

TIP TAP

The rain fell.
I watched it with my back against a wall.
Like I was about to be shot.
Like a firing squad was 20 meters away
and my last breath would be the breath of a man watching the rain.
It was a beautiful rain.
Steady. Wet.
The heartbeat of a child.
The sound it made against the new copper gutters was
    Mendelssohn.
Was Charlie Parker.
I wanted to take a picture of it.
I wanted to make a movie of the rain.
To share it with the world
but the world did not need it be shared
by me or by anyone else with a rifle.
It just fell
like it has been falling since the dawn of man.
And that's what really got me.
The dawn of people.
How a long time ago we were alive a long time ago
and it rained.
There were no gutters. No rifles. No pans of milk.
There weren't even words for rain,
in any languages
except the language of
tip tap,
tap tip.
I stood with my back against the wall
the way I imagined many of us stand with our backs against the
    wall,
many of us here and not here,
gone and not gone.

I wanted to be sad.
I wanted to be happy.
It was raining. It rained.
The rain fell and it was steady and wet,
it was a bullet.

PART 4

THE LIGHT

I spend all day getting ready for night—
the open window darkness that gives me falling leaves, broken
   bottles,
a trip down some potholed street
with no dead end sign though there should be many.

***

All day I rustle the edges of my shirts.
I pack screwdrivers into pouches.
I wind up trumpets.
The voices of the dead have begun to speak to me
with greater precision.
It's not that I listen better.
It's that there are more of them that walk the earth.

I spend all day getting ready for them
and they will never be me.
When I am one of them
I will be a flute from the 6th grade.
I played it terribly
as terrible was all I knew.
Not that I was a bad flutist.
I was not.
But when onstage with the members of the band
I faked the whole thing.
I faked Mozart and Bach.
I faked Jethro Tull.
My death will be a lie as my flute was a lie.

***

I should have been a drunk. A cab driver.

***

Today in my readiness for night
I took the car to the bank at dusk.
I could not find a song on the radio that moved me.
I did not know what I was looking for.
Something sad.
Sad cannot be found.
It has to creep onto your shoulders
and rest its head inside your head.
It has to blow you apart when your eyes are on the road.
I wanted my head to blow up in sadness
but there was only traffic.
In the congestion of rush hour
one must swallow all the exhaust.
One must undo the engine to stay in motion.

***

I am alone tonight.
There is a skylight in the house next door
that emits an orange hue.
It's the loneliest light I have known
and that house is not my house.
It is a field in winter
I stood before when I was a boy
which rose up red and white in the moon
and destroyed the world so completely
there were only the peripheral hills
in silhouette.
They rose into the sky and when I looked back at the house--
my parents inside, my sister, family friends,
bathed in yellow light--
they were farther away
than anything could be

from anything else.
How do I return? I asked myself.
I did not want to return.
I wanted to say *fuck you I love you*
and disappear with that field inside of me,
into that field,
into the life and death of a field
bathed in moonlight before the dawn.

***

All day long I spend my time getting ready for night.
For this moment.
The sky light emitting an orange light that is the moon of that
    house
buried inside an imagined shaggy rug
which smells of marijuana and burnt toast.
The dead don't live there and I don't give a shit.
I live there, in there, in here,
and I am a field.
I am flute and a drunk cabbie driving straight ahead.

***

In night there is a day,
a daylight, a light,
that you can always find
which will be a born thing,
something come out of something else—
a paper clip, a cup of tea,
a box of bottles with the labels rubbed down to glass.
You have to prepare for this light in the light
so when the darkness comes
your solitude is a beacon for others,
for someone's wayward ship on the highway

that has lost its steering, its rudder in flames
that even the concrete can't extinguish.

You have to spend your day so completely upright and on your
    knees
that when night comes
you are there to receive its darkness
as not something broken or dead but, rather,
something that has an opening for you and you go to it
and you enter.

CITRUS BOMBS OF LOVE

Me and the girls raked the shit out of the yard.
That's what I taught them to say at school
when their teachers asked what they did over the weekend.
Me and my dad and my sister
raked the shit out of the yard.
But why?
Why why why? My wife asks
when the teachers call
to let us know what went down.
Oh, I don't know, I say
and walk to the corner store to buy some beer and Cheetos,
sit at the basketball court at the local park
and listen to the lads talk smack
at the base line, the three,
the free throw.
It must be all the anger built up inside the world of men
that makes us jaw the jawness of hurt and sorrow
in our curse words of the hot tongue.
But what about the ladies?
And maybe that's the reason I teach my daughters the language of
    my youth.
So, they'll have little pissed off men inside of them
at the end of the day.
I don't want that at the end of the day and
maybe I'm the misogynist of my manhood
being a stupid father all year long?
Or, maybe I'm a guy looking for a laugh?
Or, maybe language is a better way of breaking the silence of fear
    and tenderness
than throwing a fist into a face,
a brick into a window,
a car into a ditch.
You figure it out because I can't

and the game goes late,
the lights turn on
and these guys are good.
They're sweaty and they're good
and in a perfect world
I should just shut up and let my daughters figure it out for
    themselves.
So, I go home with gum stuck to my shoe
and bring pineapples for everyone.
Little apologies of sweetness.
Little citrus bombs of love.

THE AMERICAN POLITICAL SITUATION

The crazy beautiful Russians descend on my block like seagulls on
    the trash heap.
They curse in Russian.
They park their cars in Russian.
They run down the sidewalk in Russian leaps and bounds.
I loved a Russian woman once.
Maybe she was from Ukraine.
Maybe she was from the Urals.
She broke my heart because she wanted to.
I think I still love her. If she flew down from the sky
in her seagull Russian oblong face
I would run to her and kiss the borscht out of her lips.
This summer I taught a Russian oligarch.
He did everything to hide it
but I knew. It was the grey Armani tee shirts that gave him away.
Also, his sweet face
and how many rubles passed between his teeth
when he said the words *marigold* and *Lenin*.
He lives in St. Petersburg
and when I said I want to visit St. Petersburg
he said *You can see the colored lights in the sky*
and they are my villa of everything that is Tchaikovsky.
I want to love the Russians across the street
but they drive their cars too fast into my driveway.
They make me sad and I don't know why.
My great grandmother was born in Moscow.
She was not a high-minded woman
but knew how to cook an egg.
She spoke five languages in Russian
and Yiddish
and French, in French,
before moving to Brooklyn.
She was a lunatic who stood on the balcony of her apartment

that looked over Ocean Ave.
and screamed *glavnaya* like if she screamed it long and hard enough
a boat would arrive from the old country and sail her home.
So many people in America live inside Russia now.
No one wants to admit it but they own us.
It's good to admit.
To walk across the street and get crazy with the Russians,
to throw off the shawls and boots, enter their church,
and love them like we've been a family of seagulls
flying towards the trash heap for centuries with our Russian beaks
     wide open.

HOW LUCKY WE HAVE BEEN IN BEING STUPID

We are the stupidest people on earth.
All of us.
We walk around with nuclear power plants in our pockets
and let them leak all over our legs.
Then we go outside into the sea and radioactivate the fish.
When we come home the kids are drawing with crayons on the
    floor
and it's so cute.
Until the cat has a hangover, gets his claws into the flesh and tears
    and tears
and tears.
And the guy with his lawnmower down the street
who spills his gasoline down the sewer,
he's a peach.
I was drunk, he says but we know ourselves when we see one.
When there are no more fish and the clouds have gone grey for
    good
what will be the function of love?
Will it matter that we want to jump into the pants
of the boy with purple hair who wears the Nike Airs?
Will it matter that my wife cheated on your wife and that there was
    a feather
that burned in my fingers when I touched your arm?
We are the stupidest people of all time.
All you have to do is look at an oak tree in autumn
or a cloud passing through your window.
And if you are smart, now or even before,
you'd do well to find God to save you from being dumb.
God like a stream or an eyelash, some small thing,
like a pebble.
We are the dumbest motherfuckers that I've ever met.
Every one of us.
I mean, look at the ocean.

Go to the ocean with your clothes off,
walk through the supermarkets and freeways naked
and get to the water.
Stand in front of it for a second.
It will tell you how deranged we have been.
Numbskull deranged.
And there, on the wet sand, if lucky enough, you will feel all that
    salty air breeze slip
through the colander of the beach
and touch you in that God
that you have been trying to find and have,
in this moment, found.
If you are not,
maybe some greasy monstrous sea creature
will reach its science fiction tentacle out of the waves
and spear you in the heart.
that is everyone's heart.
Our collective stupid human heart that wants, like mad,
to keep on beating
but most days, it seems,
we are just too stupid to let it.

WASTEBASKETS OF PINK

The healing guy came into the bookstore and healed all the books.
They were sad and hurt.
Some of them had band-aids on their knees.
Some of them were crying in the corner.
The healing guy rode a skateboard and ate Skittles.
They made his eyes wastebaskets of pink.
I was at the bookstore café eating a muffin.
It tasted good.
There was so much rubble and detritus.
It was like Aleppo, but worse.
There were no buildings with dead children stapled to the beams.
Just dead words or bleeding words or broken spines between the
    shelves.
I couldn't figure out what I was doing there.
I couldn't figure out what I was doing anywhere.
Then the healing guy smashed through the window,
did one of this 360 skateboard flips through the window.
He had dreads or had an afro or he was bald.
He healed all the books like they were buildings
in Aleppo
and little children stapled to beams
in Aleppo.
It was a magic trick.
It was real.
I couldn't figure out what I needed to be doing there.
I couldn't figure out what I needed to be doing anywhere.
Then I figured it out.
I washed my hair into dreads
into an afro
into a bald head.
I got myself a skateboard
and rode it all the way to Aleppo.

DISAPPEAR LIKE AN OWL
(for William Pierce)

Blessings are an easy thing. You can find them in the back of a
    UPS truck
and under the tire of the car that's been in the driveway since
    spring.
You want to unfold them like a cheap cotton towel in the linen
    closet
to give to your friend William who lost his mother;
he's down on his hands and knees, under the carpet,
looking for scraps of memory that take the shape of marbles, twigs,
    old matchboxes
that still smell of his musty family cabin near the lake.
I go down to the laundry room and search for a few in the lint
    catcher
of my Maytag dryer, then upstairs to the roof
with a ream of paper. I make paper airplanes,
tape my blessings under the wings and fly them to his house, cross-
    town, late at night
in hopes that one might land on his tongue
and disappear like an owl.
An owl is a blessing if you see one in the wild. So is the moon
when you stick your hand in your pocket for a quarter
and there it is, all that dust, those craters,
rolling around in with the keys and dollar bills.
Some people say a blessing is not a dollar bill
but I say that it is
so you can buy your children a fresh plum--forget the trip to
    Africa--
to put in a brown paper bag for school lunch.
Blessings kill you when they are trees
and when they are fried tamales your friend Juan cooked up
because he knows you like *hot.*
Cold too, and the blessing of the fight you had with your wife

over the kind of tea to brew after the kids have fallen asleep.
Blessings are easy. It's the getting to them that's the hard part,
the falling down at the sink, the getting up after a day at work.
Waking up, getting dressed, driving over the bridge
to the supermarket,
the in-between stuff of saying and saying, again,
like it was the first and only time, *I hear you.*
Who does that anymore? Says, *I hear you*
in such a way that you know that they are listening
like a mermaid or an elephant with its huge ears, with everything?
The blessing is the ear, the earlobe, the canal
with all those little hammers. That's the easy part, the God part.
The hard part, the human part,
is turning toward the person who's talking and emptying the head
of all the little men inside with their autumn rakes and iPhones,
jamming up the wires,
turning the head to say, Bill,
I have put down my pen, my razor, my hammer and scythe.
Let's sit. Let's eat. My ears are as wide open as the sky.

·

HEY ANGEL

Hey angel, where are you?
What happened to you in your over-sized sweatshirt
with the Williams College insignia on the back?
I thought we were to meet up at the Dairy Queen a few years back.
A Blizzard between us but then all the Republicans got in the way.
I'm serious; I'm not much of a political guy
but I was hoping to catch up with you tonight,
here in my toy house
on the side of a street that is south of north
and somewhere else.
There was a text from someone I did not know.
I thought it might be you but all the Neo-Nazis got in the way.
Their sticky heads and flotsam and jetsam boots.
Their tattoos that have nowhere to go.
Tonight I have nowhere to go
and I'm waiting by the black and white television.
Little secret, I still have rabbit ears for reception
and the local channels come in just fine.
They're full of game shows from 1972 and Dan Rather types.
I was hoping you'd slide through the screen,
slip out from under the rug,
and we could have tea, but the terrorists got in the way.
Their airport bombings.
Their school shootings.
Who will stop them?
I thought we could stop them together
and then Amos Oz said something about teaspoons full of water
like little anvils of peace.
I thought he was the angel and he was,
but then the dark hours interrupted
and I wanted to find you so bad
I went to my telephone
but it was broken, no surprise,

my kid said, Dad, the elephants ran over it on their way to Zaire.
Hey angel, I thought you were in Ireland
with your Irish wings
sailing between little clumps of green,
little valleys of turf,
but the bad love got in the way
the way it always gets in the way.
But it doesn't
and that is why I am sitting here in the dark
pushing back against the earth,
down on my knees,
my fingers and palms
stuck in the piss and blood and grunge
of whatever is sinister
so I can find you.
So I can push back against the wait, the waiting,
the solitude of no work
into the solitude of only work.
Hey, angel, I am on my way, wherever you are,
here I come.

HEAVEN

I can die today.
I paid the life insurance bill.
Yesterday I couldn't die.
I thought about it a lot
when I drove to Charlestown in Rhode Island.
Especially in Providence, on I-95,
with all those crazy truckers,
those burly beefy lads on motorcycles
with handlebars that lit up the air in, Fuck you, I'm badass killer
    number one.
What if they came to kill me?
What if they flew their Harley into my engine block
and the little Honda exploded?
No money for the kids, the wife,
the little cat who is fatter than us all.
I said to the clouds, I don't want to die today.
I have not paid the life insurance bill.
The clouds said, Be a bit more selfish.
So I stopped the car and got a dozen from Dunkin,
took my shirt off at the beach, made love to a seal
while tossing back a chocolate curler,
and screamed, Take me now.
But of course, no one heard me,
not the politicians, the wall street brokers,
the right wing bikers,
and my belly grew in size towards heaven.
Today, I could die and find out what heaven looks like.
I wouldn't have to worry about my premium; my wife would get
    half a mil.
In heaven I want there to be a pool
and a few white chairs with the billowy linen.
I want there to be Irish women walking around with large
    sunglasses

and pitchers of water.
That's it.
Today, I could die and have that.
I paid the life insurance bill.
In five minutes,
my friend Daniel is coming to meet me for a chat.
We'll sit on Adirondack chairs and scheme up schemes
to make cash.
We'll watch the birds and the trees and the sky
reflect its blue off the blue
off the water
that refracts into gold
and speak Spanish and English
like they are all the languages in the world
you would ever need
before you die.

A LITTLE GUT MAGIC

All my old friends are 53.
We all look 25.
I'm serious.
None of us have wrinkles the size of tomahawks.
There are no stretch marks like whales circling the waist.
There might be a little gut magic
but that's due to a donut or two,
some water weight.
I went to the reunion in my mind last night
and all of us glowed like sunlight off of autumn leaves in June.
We were the mash up of seasons.
I sat on a bench with Deborah,
she's the youngest of the lot, and said,
Remember the time when we were old
and forgot how to call ourselves
old.
She said,
We let that go years ago.
Then we held hands and did not mention a thing
except that we were thirsty for coffee and got up to get a pot.
The whole thing got me thinking:
How does the body transpose itself into youthfulness as time
marches on?
We all have one thing in common.
When we were kids
we ran around naked for hours.
We skinny dipped.
We played badminton in the nude
and sang folk songs till our lips were blue
in the middle of The Pine Woods
but didn't care
and let our voices plaster the sky with tonal deficiencies
but it did not matter,

we were naked and sang like
our songs were the only things that mattered,
like our lives depended on our voices
as they came together
and breathed gold.
It prepared us for tender faces in our Fifties.
So, here's my advice:
if you are young, go get naked with your friends and sing.
The world sucks so sing.
It does not matter what songs,
sing them into your bodies and let them be naked and kid you not
the world will take notice
and maybe, for a little while,
it won't suck so much.

ABOUT MATTHEW LIPPMAN

Matthew Lippman is the author of four poetry collections—*The New Year of Yellow* (winner of the Kathryn A. Morton Prize, Sarabande Books), *Monkey Bars, Salami Jew,* and *American Chew* (winner of the Burnside Review of Books Poetry Prize).